Wrestling

GETTING THE EDGE: CONDITIONING, INJURIES, AND LEGAL & ILLICIT DRUGS

Wrestling

by J. S. McIntosh

MC
PUBLISHERS

Mason Crest Publishers

MASON CREST PUBLISHERS INC.
370 Reed Road
Broomall, Pennsylvania 19008
(866)MCP-BOOK (toll free)
www.masoncrest.com

First Printing
9 8 7 6 5 4 3 2 1

Library of Congress Cataloging-in-Publication Data

McIntosh, J. S.
   Wrestling / by J. S. McIntosh.
        p. cm.
   Includes bibliographical references and index.
   ISBN 978-1-4222-1743-6   ISBN (series) 978-1-4222-1728-3
   1. Wrestling. I. Title.
   GV1195.M37 2011
   796.812—dc22
                                        2010017923

Produced by Harding House Publishing Service, Inc.
www.hardinghousepages.com
Interior Design by MK Bassett-Harvey.
Cover Design by Torque Advertising + Design.
Printed in the USA by Bang Printing.

The creators of this book have made every effort to provide accurate information, but it should not be used as a substitute for the help and services of trained professionals.

Contents

Introduction

Getting the Edge: Conditioning, Injuries, and Legal & Illicit Drugs is a fourteen-volume series written for young people who are interested in learning about various sports and how to participate in them safely. Each volume examines the history of the sport and the rules of play; it also acts as a guide for prevention and treatment of injuries, and includes instruction on stretching, warming up, and strength training, all of which can help players avoid the most common musculoskeletal injuries. Each volume also includes tips on healthy nutrition for athletes, as well as information on the risks of using performance-enhancing drugs or other illegal substances. Getting the Edge offers ways for readers to healthily and legally improve their performance and gain more enjoyment from playing sports. Young athletes will find these volumes informative and helpful in their pursuit of excellence.

Sports medicine professionals assigned to a sport with which they are not familiar can also benefit from this series. For example, a football athletic trainer may need to provide medical care for a local gymnastics meet. Although the emergency medical principles and action plan would remain the same, the athletic trainer could provide better care for the gymnasts after reading a simple overview of the principles of gymnastics in Getting the Edge.

Although these books offer an overview, they are not intended to be comprehensive in the recognition and management of sports injuries. They should not replace the professional advice of a trainer, doctor, or nutritionist. The text helps the reader appreciate and gain awareness of the sport's history, standard training techniques, common injuries, dietary guidelines, and the dangers of using drugs to gain an advantage. Reference material and directed readings are provided for those who want to delve further into these subjects.

Written in a direct and easily accessible style, GETTING THE EDGE is an enjoyable series that will help young people learn about sports and sports medicine.

—*Susan Saliba, Ph.D., National Athletic Trainers' Association Education Council*

1

The Basics of Wrestling

Understanding the Words

bonobos: *Apes related to chimpanzees, but having longer, more slender limbs.*

formalized: *Created an official structure for something, with defined rules and regulations.*

ideal: *The highest standard of perfection.*

ritualized: *Something that has been developed to include a certain set of behaviors, practices, movements, etc., often performed in a ceremonial manner.*

patrons: *People who support sports, arts, literature, etc., with gifts of money, material gifts, or endorsements.*

choreographed: *Planned with a series or pattern of arranged movements.*

Organized fighting without the intent of physical harm is something many mammals do. Wolves, foxes, and domestic canines—"man's best friend"—all snarl and roll around in make-believe fury, using their open mouths in a form of play-fighting. Male goats butt heads in mock competitions. Chimpanzees and bonobos, the closest evolutionary link to humans, wrestle with each other without any intent to cause harm. Scientists think that animals engage in these pretend battles to reduce tension and educate their young for the day when they may need to know real battle skills.

Humans aren't all that different. Siblings often tussle like puppies, and adults enjoy competitions of strength. Wrestling is the formalized sport that has evolved from these mock duels of strength.

Goats are just one of the many animals—including humans—that play fight.

The History of Wrestling

ANCIENT WRESTLING

We know from archeological evidence that wrestling was practiced at least 3,000 years before the birth of Christ. It was both a form of military training and also an early form of bodybuilding, a way to perfect the ideal human body. Babylonian artwork dating from the third millennium BCE depicts wrestlers grappling with each other using belt-hold grips. Similar works of art have been found in Egypt, India, Japan, China, and Europe, all dating from the centuries between 3,000 BCE and the first century bce.

Competitive wrestling is also described in ancient literature. Monumental wrestling battles are described in the Gilgamesh Epic, which was written down on stone tablets around 2,000 BCE in Mesopotamia, an ancient kingdom of the Middle East. In the Old Testament of the Bible, Abraham's grandson Jacob wrestles with an angel, who finally makes use of divine power to dislocate Jacob's hip, but even so cannot break free from Jacob's iron grip.

A few thousand years later, the ancient Greeks were also passionate about wrestling. Wrestling schools, known as *palestras*, flourished throughout ancient Greek cities, and wrestling was included in the Olympic games as early as 708 BCE. In these early Olympics, there were two main types of wrestling: *orthia pale* and *kato pale*. Orthia pale athletes fought standing, and the winner had to throw his opponent to the ground twice in three bouts. Kato pale combined what today we would consider wrestling and boxing, and the contestants fought at floor level. Victory was secured when one contestant was forced to submit, signaling defeat by raising the right hand with a pointed index finger. All wrestlers fought in the nude, and matches took place in an earthen ring called a keroma. The wrestlers' bodies were smeared with olive oil in order to make grips more difficult and to protect the skin. The Romans

Wrestling was a sport enjoyed by the ancient Greeks and portrayed in their artwork.

WRESTLING

DID YOU KNOW?

Glima is still practiced today in Denmark and Sweden, as well as Iceland, where it is the national sport. There is one difference in today's version of the sport: instead of pants, contestants wear three leather belts for grip points, one around each thigh and the other around the waist.

adopted Greek wrestling around 186 BCE, and it became a popular sport in the Roman Empire.

Ancient wrestling was a brutal affair. Death was common. Gradually the sport became safer, and the basic types of wrestling we know today were established by 1000 CE. These fell into three categories. First was the "catch hold" style, in which the wrestlers took hold of each other before officials gave the signal to fight. Second was the "loose" style, in which the contestants stood at a distance, waiting for the signal, and then rushed in to apply throws, grips, and other techniques. Third was the "belt and jacket" style, in which contestants wore special wrestling belts or clothing, which were held throughout the match and used to apply leverage. The three categories of wrestling were also subdivided into styles that permitted the use of the legs to trip and pin opponents during the fight, and those that permitted the use of arms only.

In the eighth century CE, the Japanese developed sumo wrestling, a highly ritualized martial art that is still popular in modern Japan. Sumo wrestling features *mawashi*, silk belts that are 33 feet (10 meters) long and wound around each contestant's waist. The mawashi are gripped during bouts between heavyweight competitors, each of whom can weigh as much as 440 pounds (199 kg). Bouts are won by throwing one's opponent to the ground, knocking him out of the ring, or a judge's decision.

MEDIEVAL TIMES

As a popular sporting pastime, wrestling began to decline in Europe in the fourth century CE. The collapse of the Roman Empire meant that wealthy patrons no longer supported wrestling and that locations in which large-scale public sports displays could be staged were no longer available. These changes did not mean that the sport of wrestling died out completely. Wrestling continued at a local level.

Wrestling revived and flourished, however, in different forms during medieval times. In the Middle East, wrestlers competed in *koresh*, a loose style of wrestling that originated in Turkey. In Scandinavia (the countries of Northern Europe), a type of wrestling called *glima* was popular. In this wily wrestling contest, contestants used trips and other rapid movements to throw their opponent to the ground, gripping the opponent's trouser waist for leverage. In England, wrestling was an important pastime, as well as being a practical martial skill taught to knights and other soldiers.

In medieval Europe, the ability to wrestle became the mark of a gentleman warrior, and books on wrestling techniques were required reading. Fiore dei Liberi, a fifteenth-century medieval swordsman from the Italian town of Cividale del Friuli, wrote one of the most influential of these books, called *Flos Duellatorum*, in which he outlined a system of unarmed combat for use in warfare and self-defense. His writings became popular reading for gentlemen throughout Europe. In addition to wrestling techniques, Fiore de Liberi also explained how to fight using sticks, swords, and other weapons.

THE BIRTH OF MODERN WRESTLING

Wrestling continued as a military activity and a form of entertainment for centuries. Its development into the modern sport began in the eighteenth century in Europe, where the growing popularity of circuses gave wrestlers a public showcase for their talents. Wrestlers often challenged a member of the public to wrestle them for a cash reward, beating most opponents by using brutal techniques.

European immigrants to the United States brought wrestling with them. They found that the sport was already in North America, popular among

Native Americans. For white men, as in Europe, the sport was initially concentrated at fairs, carnivals, and circuses.

By the late nineteenth century, wrestling became more professional. Two
styles emerged that form the foundation of wrestling today. The Greco-
Roman style applied to grips only above the waist. Use of the legs was not

*The medieval form of wrestling called glima survived in Iceland through the twentieth century,
and is still practiced today.*

permitted for pinning or gripping the opponent. Matches began from a standing position or with the two wrestlers crouching on all fours on the floor. This style originated in France and tended to be concentrated in mainland Europe. Meanwhile, freestyle wrestling became more popular in the United Kingdom and United States. This style allowed the use of legs and resulted in more dramatic displays of technique. In both styles, the objective was (and still is) to throw and pin an opponent, winning by submission or a judge's decision.

By the end of the nineteenth century, both Greco-Roman and freestyle wrestling had been accepted as professional sports. In 1888, the Amateur Athletic Association (AAA) of the United States acknowledged wrestling to be an official sport, and U.S. national championships were held that same year in New York. Greco-Roman wrestling was featured in the 1896 Olympics, and the Federation Internationale de Lutte Amateur (FILA, the International Amateur Wrestling Federation) was formed in 1912 to oversee international wrestling competitions, including the Olympics. The same year, the National Collegiate Athletic Association (NCAA) held its first wrestling championship in Ames, Iowa. In 1920, the Olympics featured freestyle wrestling.

Starting with the 1920s, however, professional wrestling increasingly became overshadowed by boxing, becoming more of an entertainment than a sport. Wrestlers began to adopt heroic or villainous roles, and fights, which were choreographed like dances, had a foregone conclusion. This type of wrestling is dominant today. The World Wrestling Federation (WWF) entertains millions around the world with larger-than-life characters who take part in theatrical combat.

Traditional wrestling, however, is far from dead. In 1928, the NCAA developed rules for the collegiate style of wrestling and set out a definitive system of rules and scoring for collegiate competitions in the United States. During the 1960s, the United States Wrestling Federation (USWF) was formed outside the AAA in order to promote amateur wrestling. The NCAA standardized

GEORGE HACKENSCHMIDT VS. FRANK GOTCH

One of the most famous bouts in wrestling history took place in April 1908, at the World Heavyweight Championships. Frank Gotch, the formidable farm boy from Iowa, met the champion George Hackenschmidt, who was known as the "Russian Lion" and was the clear favorite to win. Indeed, many feared that Gotch would not survive because of the ferocity of Hackenschmidt's bear hug. However, after a brutal two-hour match in Chicago, Gotch clamped Hackenschmidt in a scorching toehold that forced the "Lion" to submit. (Gotch had proved in the past that he could break his opponent's legs with such a technique.) After the match, there were claims that Gotch had used illegal moves to win the fight. Yet Gotch also won the rematch with Hackenschmidt in 1911, with a clear two falls out of three. The battles between these two giants of the ring led to a major surge of interest in wrestling in the United States and helped form the vibrant amateur sport that exists today.

rules for international and national amateur competitions in 1967. In 1969 the USWF held its first National Open Championships in Evanston, Illinois. Finally, the USWF became U.S.A. Wrestling (USAW) in 1983 and took over as the national governing body for wrestling in the United States.

Since the 1960s, wrestling has become a major sport in high schools and colleges throughout the United States. Although amateur wrestling does not have the same massive budget as entertainment wrestling, it is still a popular sport and produces talented fighters every year. In the international arena, the United States has been a powerful force in wrestling for decades. Since 1983, wrestlers in USAW alone have won twenty-seven Olympic medals (fourteen gold) and sixty-seven World championship medals (twenty-one gold).

Wrestling has become a popular high school sport.

Wrestling Rules

Modern amateur wrestling bouts take place in a circular area 23 feet (7 m) in diameter, set in a 39-by-39-foot (about 12-by-12 m) section of matting.

A bout usually consists of two three-minute periods (a thirty-second rest is given between the periods). During these times, the wrestler will attempt to throw his opponent down and pin his shoulders to the ground. If the opponent can be immobilized in this way for several seconds, the referee will count it as a "fall" and award the bout to the dominant wrestler. If no fall is achieved, the winner is decided on a points basis.

The referee will give points for various successful attacks or defenses, scoring on technical ability and the control of the contest. By wearing a red armband on one arm and a blue armband on another, the referee shows who has scored the points, and he uses his fingers to show the number of points scored.

Judges seated at the side of the mat have the ability to question the scoring or award points of their own. If the referee and a judge are in disagreement, a mat chairman will resolve the issue.

Opportunities to Wrestle

Few individuals manage to make a living from wrestling. Most professional wrestlers are concentrated in entertainment wrestling, and the ultimate goal for a college wrestler is to enter the U.S. National Team and represent his country.

For many young people, wrestling is a high school or college sport that provides entertainment and challenges in addition to their academic studies. Many schools and colleges have their own wrestling teams and dedicated coaches. These allow students not only to learn wrestling but also to compete in the different local, regional, state, and even national competitions held throughout the United States each year.

WRESTLING

Wrestling competitions are organized according to age divisions and weight categories. These can vary according to the organization running the competition. U.S.A. Wrestling—the main governing body for wrestling in the United States—currently has nine age categories, beginning at the age of seven:

- Bantam, 7–8 years
- Midget, 9–10 years
- Novice, 11–12 years
- Schoolboy/girl, 13–14 years
- Cadet, 15–16 years
- Junior, 17–20 years
- FILA Junior World, 17–20 years
- University, 18–24 (men); 17–24 (women)
- Senior, 18+ (men); 17+ (women)

In terms of weight, categories in the schoolboy division and above are: 75, 83, 90, 95, 100, 105, 110, 115, 120, 125, 130, 135, 140, 145, 152, 160, 171, 189, and 250 pounds.

Contestants wrestle only with those in their own weight category. This can cause great stress for a young wrestler, since being at the top of your weight category gives you a competitive advantage. Many wrestlers attempt to lose weight and place themselves in the top of the next category down, rather than wrestle with big opponents in their original category. Taking drastic measures to lose weight quickly before a match is not a healthy practice. Young adults need to remember that good wrestlers defeat larger opponents with superior technique, not just sheer bulk.

TRAINING CAMPS AND COLLEGES

When selecting a college or university to further their education, some wrestling students deliberately choose those with strong wrestling teams. Colleges with good wrestling squads and coaches are scattered throughout the United States but many are found in the Midwest. The most consistently successful colleges are in Iowa, Oklahoma, and Nebraska, as well as Pennsylvania in the Northeast. The Oklahoma State University wrestling team (the "Cowboys"), coached by the legendary wrestler John Smith, often competes in five or six wrestling competitions each month. The university also hosts residential John Smith Wrestling Camps.

In wrestling, contestants only compete against wrestlers who are in their same weight category. Always rely on technique rather than weight to win a match.

WRESTLING

JOHN SMITH

John Smith ranks as one of the greatest wrestlers in U.S. history. His achievements are almost unrivaled. At the national level, he has won five U.S. National titles and his international achievements are just as impressive, including two Olympic gold medals, two Goodwill Games gold medals, and six straight World Championship golds. In 1992 he was awarded the title of Wrestler of the Year by the international governing body of amateur wrestling, the **Federation International de Lutte Amateur** (FILA). In 1987, he was inducted into the National Wrestling Hall of Fame and the Oklahoma Hall of Fame. For many years, he has coached the immensely successful Oklahoma Cowboys team, which produced national and international champions. His coaching credentials also include the 2000 Olympic Team in Sydney, Australia.

Wrestling camps are a good way to push your technique forward, prepare yourself for competitions, and even be selected for regional, state, or national teams. Courses range from single-day master classes to two-week courses. A two-week course is extremely demanding. It can involve four physical workouts each day, including sessions of flexibility training, weight lifting, and running, as well as wrestling. Camps also give competitors the opportunity to wrestle with teams from around the United States, and so provide excellent tournament preparation.

Saori Yoshida cheers from her coach's shoulders after winning the 55-kg Olympic female wrestling final at the Beijing 2008 Olympics.

NATIONAL TEAMS

If you are a truly talented and dedicated wrestler, you can work through the many levels of local, regional, state, interstate, and national competitions to eventually try out for the U.S. National Team.

The first stage on this long journey is to win in your weight class in the U.S. National Championships. Any wrestler is eligible to compete in the National Championships as long as he or she falls within the right age and weight

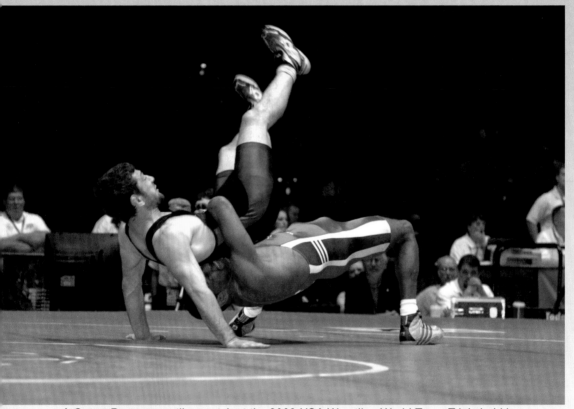

A Greco-Roman wrestling match at the 2003 USA Wrestling World Team Trials held in Indianapolis, Indiana.

categories and holds a USA Wrestling membership card, which provides insurance in case of injury. In addition, all wrestlers must pass a physical examination to check that they are not carrying any infectious skin diseases.

The Nationals are a huge competition, with Greco-Roman and freestyle events for both teams and individuals. Runner-up, finalists, and medal winners may have the opportunity to go for the U.S. World Team Trials. Every year, the World Team Trials are held to determine the Olympic, World Championship, and Pan-American wrestling team for the United States.

Strict rules govern who can enter the World Team Trials. The wrestlers must be over seventeen and have placed in the top seven of their weight class at the U.S. National Championship. Those who come in first in the Nationals go on to the finals of the World Team Trials, where they meet the winners in the weight class from the challenge Tournament. The overall winners are then selected for the U.S. team who then go on to compete in the international stage.

It is a long and difficult road to reach such high levels in the world of wrestling. Many other wrestling challenges exist at local and regional levels, and these can be just as rewarding. Each wrestler must look after her own health and properly care for any injuries suffered. Ignoring injuries is a good way to cut short your wrestling career, so make sure you invest in your safety. Learn how to prepare for your sport, both mentally and physically.

2
Mental Preparation and Safety Equipment

Understanding the Words

stamina: *The ability of the body to keep going, despite tiredness, injury, or illness.*

flexibility: *The ability of the body to be easily bent and moved without injury.*

regimen: *A planned program of diet and exercise.*

pain threshold: *The amount of pain a person can withstand.*

resilient: *Capable of recovering quickly after pain, injury, or other setbacks.*

exploited: *Used selfishly for one's own purposes.*

optimum: *The best and most favorable.*

singlets: *Tight, one-piece outfits worn by wrestlers.*

ligaments: *Bands of tissue connecting bones to each other.*

During any particular wrestling season, about 50 percent of amateur wrestlers will be injured. A recent survey of a single wrestling season found 219 injuries among a total of 458 wrestlers.

Wrestling is a "violent" sport that uses pain to inflict defeat upon the opponent. As a result, injuries should be expected. However, your mental attitude can make a difference.

Self-Control

The first principle of mental preparation is self-control. Be clear in your own mind which techniques you can use and which are beyond your skill level—and don't yield to the temptation to try something that is beyond your current abilities. Controlling an opponent who is vigorously resisting your actions requires fast, powerful, and skillful techniques, rather than just brute force. Many young wrestlers want to apply advanced techniques well before they are physically capable of doing so. Be particularly careful if you have been reading wrestling books. Unless they are written for beginners, wrestling books may contain a large number of advanced moves aimed at a more experienced audience. Do not attempt to apply these techniques without first running them past your coach. A difficult hip toss or double-leg tackle could overload your back muscles and result in injury if your body is not well trained.

In cooperation with your coach, set up a disciplined regimen of training to take you in sequence from the most basic of techniques to the most advanced. For competitions or sparring sessions, use only those techniques that are so familiar that they come naturally. Be prepared to progress slowly, learning one step at a time. To avoid frustration, look back to when you began, remembering what you have achieved since then. Also, if the only technique you know is a front headlock, aim to be the best at front headlocks! It is better to know a few techniques well than many techniques badly.

A good wrestler has a strong, athletic physique and high levels of stamina and flexibility. Remember, the better your physical condition, the less likely you are to be injured. This requires self-discipline; it means hours of physical training on top of the time you spend wrestling. Self-discipline does not come naturally to many people. You may be tempted to skip training sessions for what seems like very good reasons or stop working on flexibility because

Since wrestling uses pain to defeat an opponent, mental training is important.

progress is frustratingly slow. If you stick with the regimen, however, you will find that both your muscles and your self-discipline will consistently grow!

Increase Your Self-Discipline

Here are some ways to increase your self-discipline:

- Set realistic training goals and specific days or times for completing them. By meeting each goal, you become more capable of setting higher standards for yourself.

- Do not lose sight of what you are trying to achieve. Everything that is worth achieving takes effort, and all the world's great wrestlers have had to go through exactly the same process of development. Picture your own goal—such as being a local or national champion—before, during, and after every training session.

- Reward yourself every time you meet one of your training goals. Do this in whatever way you like best: by going out with friends, listening to music, or watching a movie. Be careful, though, about rewarding yourself with food—you could undo all the good work of your training session.

- Tell yourself that the ability to work hard is a gift, not a chore—without hard work, your dreams will remain only dreams.

If you keep to a strict regimen of training, your wrestling skills improve, and you will develop self-respect. Be honest about your capabilities. Wrestling requires a confident attitude, not an arrogant one. Trying to fight beyond your capabilities will result in injury and discouragement. Also be sure to avoid training when you are tired, hungry, or suffering from illness. You might want to push yourself during these times, but doing so will only expose you to injury or further illness as your body attempts to perform in its weakened state.

A Strong Mind

There is no way around the fact that wrestling involves pain. Ironically, however, raising your mental pain threshold can help to prevent injuries rather than expose you to more. Wrestlers with a low pain threshold are more likely

Raising your mental pain threshold can keep you from panicking during a match—which will ultimately help you to avoid injuries.

to panic if a fight is not going their way, and so they may make mistakes that result in injury.

Raising your pain threshold begins by experiencing pain itself. Whenever you experience pain during a wrestling bout, tell yourself mentally that you can handle it and that you are not going to quit. Of course, you are right to submit if the pain is excruciating, but if you feel that you can endure it, then hang on. Practice speaking positively to yourself, even when a situation seems desperate, and keep thinking clearly about how you can escape or fight back. Focus all your energy on winning the fight rather than simply surviving it. A winning attitude is tough and resilient; any weakness will be found by your opponent and mercilessly exploited. Having a strong mind will also make your body produce its optimum performance, and so provide the strength to resists attacks that might produce injury.

Equipment

Many wrestling competitions take place with almost no protective clothing. Yet for certain styles of collegiate wrestling and for training, there is a useful range of safety gear to shield you from serious injury.

A popular piece of safety equipment is a set of ear guards. During sparring, ears can be torn, crushed, or bruised from powerful headlocks and grips. Years ago, many seasoned wrestlers had characteristic "cauliflower" ears, but modern ear guards protect against this injury. Worn over the head, a set of ear guards consists of a fabric sling containing two foam ear pads that fit snugly to the side of the head. These will protect the ears during even the hardest clashes and prevent tearing, but make sure that your coach helps you fit the guards properly before you spar. Ear guards usually cost about twenty to thirty dollars, but you may be able to buy them more cheaply through your team.

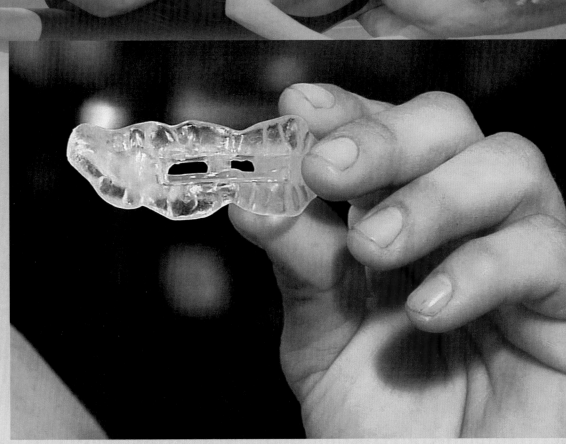

A mouth guard protects your upper teeth from injury.

Another important piece of equipment is a mouth guard, designed to protect the vulnerable top row of your teeth. Mouth guards are often optional in wrestling competitions and at gyms, but they are most definitely a good idea: they will keep you from losing teeth if you are hit by the opponent's elbow or head, or if you strike your mouth on the floor during sparring. The most basic mouth guard is one you fit yourself. This is a jaw-shaped piece of plastic, which softens when placed in boiling water. You put the softened mouth guard onto your top set of teeth and suck it hard so that it molds itself to the

WRESTLING MATS

The proper care of wrestling mats is important for your general safety during training and competition.

- Make sure that there are no gaps between the mats. Gaps can result in sprained ankles if feet slip into them. Mat tape is available to secure the mats to one another and also to make repairs of any tears in the fabric.
- Clean up any sweat or water from mats between sparring to prevent slipping.
- At the end of the day, the mats should be cleaned with proper antifungal and anti-bacterial mat cleaner to stop the transference of skin problems between athletes. The underside of the mats must be cleaned at least once a week.
- If you have to clean up blood, wear rubber gloves. First soak up the blood with paper towels, then clean the area with disinfectant.

shape of your teeth. Once it cools, it will retain a personal fit to your mouth. When fitting these mouth guards, always be careful that you do not burn your mouth on any boiling water that is trapped in the shield.

Another option is to have your dentist make a professional mouth guard for you. A cast is taken of your mouth, and a mouth guard is then made to this model. The mouth guard will be fitted properly so that it is exactly contoured around every tooth. A professional mouth guard can even be fitted for a fixed brace. There are also mouth guards that protect both the top and bottom sets of teeth. These are fitted with ventilation holes so that breathing is not affected, but many wrestlers prefer not to wear such a large piece of plastic in the mouth.

BASIC OUTFIT

When it comes to your outfit, most sports stores will sell wrestling singlets. These are usually made of nylon, Lycra, or a similar flexible material. There should be no constricting material around the shoulders or arms; you need to be able to move as freely as possible during sparring matches. Although you can train in regular T-shirts and shorts, this is not advisable. Such clothing is not designed for the rigors of wrestling and is likely to be torn.

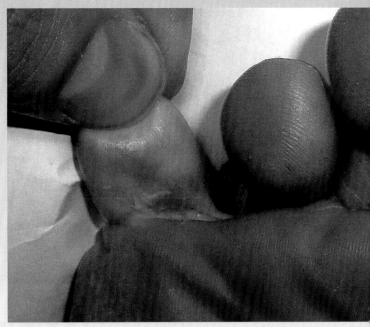

You should buy two or three singlets if you are going to practice wrestling seriously (singlets range in cost between twenty and ninety dollars). Wash the singlet after each training session. A build-up of sweat— both yours and that of your competitor—will encourage

Athlete's foot is one of the fungal skin conditions that can be caught from wrestling mats if they are not regularly cleaned with an antifungal cleanser.

VISUALIZATION

Professionals in almost every sport benefit from visualization. Basically, this means training your imagination. Researchers have discovered that athletes who spend time imagining that they are doing well at their sport actually improve more quickly than those who concentrate only on physical development. They are also better at acquiring new skills. Visualization also helps to prevent injuries by improving technique. For wrestling, here is how visualization could work:

- Find a quiet place, away from other people, where you can sit still or lie down. Close your eyes.
- Relax your body by focusing on the ebb and flow of your breathing. At the same time, imagine each muscle of your body softening like butter on a warm windowsill, working from your toes to your scalp.

skin problems such as rashes, infections, and even localized skin diseases. Washing out your wrestling gear between each training session will help to protect both you and your opponents.

If you have injured or weak knees—a common complaint among dedicated wrestlers—you can help to prevent further damage by wearing knee protectors. Good knee protectors are made from thick neoprene, an elas-

- Imagine performing a technique that you are currently learning. Even if you cannot perform the technique yet, imagine yourself doing it perfectly, throwing or pinning your opponent with total confidence. Mentally rehearse the technique yet again; imagine yourself doing it perfectly, throwing or pinning your opponent with total confidence. Mentally rehearse the technique time and time again, starting off slowly, and then building up speed and power.
- The key to visualization is imagining everything in detail. See the picture in color, and notice details about your surroundings, such as noise, items of equipment, the appearance of your opponent, and so on. A clear picture will make the mental training more realistic.
- Once you have rehearsed the technique in your imagination, take three deep breaths. On the third breath, open your eyes.

ticized material with excellent supportive and protective properties. The basic knee protector is a neoprene sheath that is worn around the knee. It has two main benefits: it holds the knee cap and ligaments of the knee and stabilizes them against further injuries during twisting or pushing actions; and it disperses the force of blows to your knee away from your knee cap, lessening any damage.

WRESTLING

If you know you have a weak knee, wearing a knee protector, like the one worn by the wrestler here, can protect you against further injuries.

Shoes are one of the most important pieces of wrestling equipment. Try to invest in proper wrestling shoes rather than general trainers, which are unsuited to handling the pressures of wrestling activity. Wrestling shoes have several features that help prevent injury to the feet and ankles: They have high ankle support to grip the ankle and make it less vulnerable to twisting and sprains. The sole of the shoe will often have a split design so that the shoe can cope with the flexing demands placed on it when the wrestler is pushing or squatting.

3
Preparing the Body

Understanding the Words

endurance: *The ability to keep going despite difficulties.*

dislocations: *Injuries that move the bones out of their proper places.*

fractures: *Breaks, such as in bones.*

antagonistic: *Pairs of muscle groups that work together by performing opposite actions, such as flexing and extending.*

laterals: *Short for* latissimus dorsi, *the pair of large triangular muscles covering the middle and lower back.*

quadriceps: *The large muscle on the front of the thigh.*

hamstrings: *The group of muscles at the back of the thigh and behind the knee.*

Wrestling places tough demands upon strength, endurance, and flexibility. Inexperienced wrestlers will too often concentrate only on developing their strength, while neglecting their endurance and flexibility, and so expose themselves to injury. Two main types of injury occur during wrestling.

The first type involves impact injuries, which happen when wrestlers' bodies collide or when wrestlers are hurled violently to the ground. Causes of impact injuries include head butts (which constitute about 30 percent of all wrestling injuries); fingers in eyes; elbows in faces; and hard throws onto the back, hip, or shoulder.

The second type involves twisting or wrenching injuries. Many wrestling techniques are aimed at bending body joints against the natural limits of their movement, to inflict pain while establishing control of the opponent. Alternatively, they may be designed to throw the opponent with sudden explosive movements. Both types of technique can result in a variety of injuries. These include strains, dislocations, torn ligaments or muscles, and even fractures. Injuries are much more likely to occur in athletes who have poor flexibility or weak muscle tone.

Flexibility

Flexible wrestlers are much more likely to withstand injuries. Their muscles and ligaments have greater elasticity, and so are less likely to strain or tear when put through extreme ranges of movement. For wrestlers, the most vulnerable areas in terms of strain are the back, neck, shoulders, hips, knees, and ankles. A wrestler's flexibility training should aim to increase the flexibility of these areas to their maximum extent. When you warm up for sparring, use stretches that specifically target these areas, and use them in dedicated stretching sessions at least three times a week. The following are just a few examples:

The more flexible you are, the less apt you are to be injured when performing holds like that shown here.

ANKLE STRETCH

While sitting down, put the left ankle on top of the right knee. Hold the raised ankle with your left hand, and take hold of the toes and the ball of the foot with your right hand. Using your right hand, circle the foot around in one direction in large circles, repeating ten times before turning it in the opposite direction. Then pull your foot up, stretching it toward your shin. Hold the stretch and breathe out. Finally, pull the foot in a stretch away from the shin. Repeat for the other foot.

LEG STRETCH

Sit on the floor with both legs straight out in front of you. Draw one leg in so that the sole of the foot sits against the inner thigh of the extended leg. Sit up straight and breathe in deeply, then exhale slowly and bend forward from the hips and waist over your extended leg until you can grip your foot. Slowly pull on the toes so that the heel lifts slightly off the floor. You should feel a deep stretch along the back of the leg and knee. Finally, lower the heel to the floor and sit up.

HIP STRETCH

Stand upright with your legs in a wide "A" shape about two shoulder-widths apart. Bend forward from the waist, and take your body weight on your hands. Now slowly sink your hips downward, inching your legs wider and wider apart. Keep breathing deeply as you do this, and go down only as far as you can manage. When you are at your limit, hold the position for five to ten seconds, and try to relax your muscles. You may find that you can go down a little farther after doing this. When you have reached your maximum stretch, come out of the stretch by walking your feet inward (while maintaining your weight on your hands) until you are able to stand up.

BACK STRETCH

Remember: do not put any weight on your head—doing this makes you run the risk of a neck injury. Lie on your back. Draw your legs up so that your feet are flat on the floor near your buttocks. Place your hands on either side of your neck with your fingers under the shoulders, pointing down your body. Breathe in, then push with your feet and hands, and raise your abdomen

A "bridge" is a good stretch for your back muscles.

WRESTLING

toward the ceiling. You should end up in an arched shape, a stretch usually known as "a bridge." Hold the stretch for a few seconds, and then lower yourself back down to the starting position. Repeat two more times.

If you do not have the power to lift yourself up, have a partner support your inner back throughout this stretch. This stretch is ideal for developing the "bridge" position used to resist a fall.

NECK STRETCH

Stand upright, facing forward. Pull your chin down to your chest and hold for a couple of seconds, then rock your head backward and look up at the ceiling, stretching the neck upward while you do so. Repeat this set of stretches three times. Then twist your head to the left and right (five times on each side), stretching the neck to the fullest extent. Finally, rotate your head in large circles, remembering to pull you head up rather than back at the top of each circle.

STRETCHING RULES

These are just a few of the stretches you have to do to maximize your flexibility. Whatever stretch you are doing, obey these important rules:

- Stop if you experience any sharp or burning pains.

- Do not attempt to rush flexibility—stretching too hard will just result in an injury.

- Do not bounce yourself deeper into the stretch. Jerking movements increase the possibility of muscle or ligament injury.

- Practice flexibility training regularly, at least every other day. You will soon notice a genuine improvement in your flexibility.

- Always warm up before stretching. Do some light exercise, such as fast walking or very light running, to raise your body temperature. Circle your hips and swing your arms to loosen the major joints and

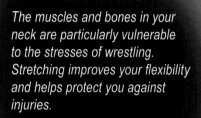

The muscles and bones in your neck are particularly vulnerable to the stresses of wrestling. Stretching improves your flexibility and helps protect you against injuries.

WRESTLING

shake out any stiffness. Warm muscles respond much better to stretching than cold muscles, and are less likely to be injured.

• Do not stretch a limb or area that is suffering from an injury.

Your coach should give you a flexibility program custom-made to your physical needs. If you have any questions, do not hesitate to ask.

Strength Training

Strength training is essential for a wrestler. Not only does it help you competitively, but it also guards you against injury. Strong muscles are less likely to be strained or torn than weak ones, and they also help to prevent dislocations of the joints by holding the joint firmly in place.

Strength training can be done without weights by using age-old techniques such as pushups, crunches, and lunges. For stomach conditioning, use crunches rather than sit-ups. During crunches, you curl your body up off the floor, but keep the small of your back on the floor. This is healthier for you than sit-ups; recent research indicates that sit-ups place too much strain on the lower spine and back muscles. Strength training with weights is a more scientific method of isolating individual muscle groups. (For a more detailed look at weight training, see *Sports Injuries: Weight Training* in this series.) Use free weights in particular. Free weights train your balance as well as build up your muscular strength. Your coach should be able to explain a full program of weight training to develop your physique. Here we can look at some general principles of strength training to help protect your body from injury:

• Establish a regular routine for weight training. Wrestlers often concentrate on strength training during the off-season, when they are able to give more time to the discipline. The important point is that the training is regular and disciplined. The ideal is about seventy-five minutes, three times a week. You can train more than that, but leave at least three days of the week for rest so that your body can recover.

Using free weights is a good way to build the muscle strength you need for wrestling.

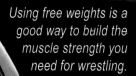

• During the weight-training session, it is vital that you exercise pairs of muscles rather than single muscles. For example, on the inside of the upper arm is the biceps and on the outside is the triceps, which is more likely to be injured. Giving equal attention to both biceps and triceps produces a stable muscle system in the arm.

The principle of working with pairs of muscle groups applies throughout the body. Opposing muscle groups are known technically as "antagonistic" muscle groups, and there are four main ones which require exercising: chest and laterals; biceps and triceps; abdominals and lower back muscles; and quadriceps and hamstrings. Be particularly careful not to develop your abdominal muscles at the expense of your back muscles. Strong abdominal muscles may be attractive to look at, but you will quickly forget this if you happen to pull your back in a wrestling match.

Weight machine features can help you build leg muscles.

PRIORITY MUSCLE GROUPS FOR WRESTLERS

- Neck muscles—some gyms will have weight machines specifically designed to strengthen the neck muscles on all four sides.
- Mid-section muscles—wrestlers require very strong abdominal and lower-back muscle to apply twisting and turning techniques. Practice regular and oblique stomach crunches; these are like sit-ups, performed straight or to each side of the body. Alternatively, use the rotary torso machine feature in most gyms.
- Leg muscles—strengthen these by performing leg-press, leg-extension, and leg-curl exercises on weight machines. Alternatively, hold a pair of dumbbells down by your sides and practice lunges: step forward deeply with one leg, then step back, alternating between legs.
- Hands and forearms—strong finger, hand, wrist, and forearm muscles are vital for gripping and controlling an opponent. There are various pieces of equipment for strengthening grip, including a simple pair of spring-loaded grip trainers.

While weight training, you should always have an expert trainer with you to help you avoid injury and to make sure you develop your body correctly. What is most important is to learn a good technique; otherwise you are likely to injure yourself. Increase the loads you lift very gradually, building up your strength slowly rather than attempting to push too far ahead. Remember, being muscular will not in itself win a wrestling match. Only technique can do that.

Endurance Training

Wrestlers are some of the fittest athletes in the world, because wrestling exercises every muscle group in the body. A wrestler with low

Make bicycling a part of your workout routine to build your aerobic endurance.

endurance, however, will soon tire and will also be vulnerable to injury. Many injuries occur when people weaken through fatigue, and this is far more likely to happen in an unfit athlete.

Build up your endurance by mixing your training with regular aerobic exercises. Aerobic exercises are those that raise the heart rate and breathing, requiring more oxygen throughout the body to fuel the effort. Typical examples include running, cycling, and swimming. Try to incorporate all three in your training regime.

Running is probably the best overall method for increasing endurance. Try to run three times a week. If you are new to running, maintain a light pace for about twenty to thirty minutes. As you become more fit, increase the length of time that you run. Set your runs in time, not distance. If you measure in distance, the tendency will be to exercise for shorter periods of time as you become fitter. Instead, work on trying to run a greater distance in the same time as your last run. During your long-distance run, insert thirty-second bursts of speed running. The speed runs train your heart and respiration to reach maximum output while already working hard. Also practice short sprints of 100 to 200 yards (about 90 to 180 m) with rest periods in between. Your basic aim while running is to raise your heartbeat to around 150 beats per minute and to keep it there for at least fifteen minutes. You can buy a simple electronic wristband that displays your heart rate while running. Be sure to invest in good running shoes that provide plenty of ankle support and grip, and alternate between running on road surfaces and soft surfaces, such as grass and earth. These measures will help to guard against conditions such as shin splints, stress fractures, and muscle strains.

Wrestling is a sport requiring both sudden explosions of effort and arduous feats of endurance. By paying attention to all aspects of your fitness, your body will be far better able to resist both sudden and gradual injuries. But injuries will still occur sometimes—so it's important to know how to handle them.

4

Common Injuries, Treatment, & Recovery

Understanding the Words

physical therapy: *The treatment of an injury or illness using physical techniques such as massage and stretching, rather than medicines or surgery.*

chronic fatigue: *Severe tiredness that continues for a long time and is not cured by rest.*

anti-inflammatory: *Medications that reduce swelling in an injury.*

mobility: *The ability to move easily.*

degeneration: *The process in which a part of the body becomes unhealthy, loses function, and begins to break down.*

traction: *A medical procedure for straightening broken bones or putting dislocated joints back into place. It involves pulling gently but firmly on a broken or dislocated limb until it goes back into its proper place.*

tendons: *Tough cords of tissue connecting muscles to bones.*

rehabilitation: *The process of restoring something, such as a part of the body, to health and proper function.*

ultrasound: *Sound waves that are outside the range of human hearing. Physical therapists sometimes use ultrasound machines to treat damaged muscles by sending the sound waves vibrating through the injured area.*

No matter how well prepared wrestlers are, both mentally and physically, injuries are a reality that is hard to totally avoid.

Neck Injuries

In wrestling, the neck is exposed to fairly extreme forces. It has to maintain the weight of the head during high impacts and harsh twisting movements. Not surprisingly, it is one of the most easily injured body areas in the sport.

Many neck injuries are the result of nerves being trapped, squeezed, or stretched during sparring. The typical symptoms of such injuries are:

- An intense pain or ache in the neck, aggravated by movement. Sometimes the pain is not sensed until the head is moved, at which point there is a burning or stinging pain in the neck. The pain may extend down through the shoulder and into the arm, or may be confined to the neck area alone.

- Sensations of numbness, pins and needles, or weakness in the arms or hands.

- Pain in the neck, resulting in headaches and nausea.

- Inability to sleep due to difficulty in getting the head into a comfortable position.

- Neck muscles that spasm, and limited mobility in the neck.

Many of these symptoms may last only a few minutes from the moment of injury before the pain dissolves and everything returns to normal. If the pain continues longer and is confined to the neck alone, take painkillers and apply heat-generating ointments or ice packs (whichever provides the best relief). Stop training and give your neck plenty of rest. With such treatment, the problem should get better within a week.

If not, see a doctor. Get professional help earlier if the pain is radiating out into both arms, or if you lost consciousness at the time of the injury. These symptoms can suggest serious injuries to the spine or an impairment of the spinal column, so a quick diagnosis is vital. If the problem is simply a

Neck pain is often the result of nerves having been stretched or pinched during sparring.

If you think you may have a whiplash injury, you should see a doctor and get an X-ray to determine the extent of the damage to your neck.

pinched nerve, the physician will probably continue the treatment you are already doing, or she may give you a neck collar or recommend some **physical therapy** to relocate the nerves.

In addition to the nerves, the ligaments, muscles, and bones of the neck may be damaged at moments of high impact. Simple neck sprains or strains have similar symptoms to pinched nerves, with the possibility of other symptoms such as a sore throat or **chronic fatigue**. After the injury, apply ice packs to the injured area two or three times a day, for up to three days, to reduce swelling. Keep the ice packs on for no more than twenty minutes (any more and you run the risk of frostbite). After this, use heat ointments and **anti-inflammatory** medicines. Remember that a bad neck sprain can take more than a month to heal. Always visit a doctor for a proper diagnosis if the pain is particularly severe or the injury is affecting the arms and shoulders.

A more serious neck injury is whiplash. Whiplash occurs when the neck is put through a traumatic flexing motion. It is an injury usually associated with automobile accidents and can be extremely serious. There will be an immediate vise-like pain in the neck, and the neck may become completely immobile. The pain of whiplash often extends up into the head and drives downward between the shoulder blades, out into the arms, and into the lower back. The injured person may experience nausea, dizziness, blurred vision, mood swings, and severe headaches. Without proper treatment, he can suffer from back troubles and neck pain for the rest of his life.

Professional medical help is required immediately after whiplash. An ambulance should be called in severe cases. X-rays or other scans will produce an accurate diagnosis. Treatment varies according to severity. For minor whiplash, the doctor may fit a collar or, alternatively, recommend complete rest. However, doctors have recently begun to recommend letting the neck move, believing this to be a better route to recovery.

After about a week of complete rest, gently practice light exercises to loosen your neck, such as making small circles with the head or writing the alphabet in the air with your nose. For more severe whiplash, radical physical therapy and even surgery may be required. Follow your doctor's advice to the letter: do not be tempted to return to wrestling until you are fully recovered with pain-free, full movement of the neck.

Back Injuries

Back injuries are another problem for wrestlers. Wrestling movements rely on sudden explosions of twisting, pushing, or lifting. All such movements can result in muscle strain or rupture in the back, or even damage to the spinal column itself. Proper strength and flexibility training and correct technique will go a long way toward preventing back injuries. Yet backs often do become weaker with age and more prone to injury.

The symptoms of muscle strain or rupture in the back are fairly obvious: the athlete will experience severe pain in the back muscles, which will be made worse through movement or lifting. Mobility in the back and neck will be reduced.

The best treatment is an initial period of complete rest. Controlling the pain is possible through pain killing and anti-inflammatory medication (available from either your doctor or drugstore).

As the initial strain becomes bearable, introduce light exercise to increase the back's flexibility and strength. For about a week, do gentle backstretches, such as the standing side bend. Then perform light warm-up routines and the lightest of weight-training exercises with small weight loads.

Work on sitting and standing with correct posture. The back should be straight with the shoulders drawn backward; imagine that you are being drawn up straight via a rope attached to the top of your head. Take hot baths to apply heat treatment to injured muscles.

SLIPPED DISK

A classic problem for wrestlers is known as the "slipped disk," professionally known as a "herniated disk." A herniated disk occurs when degeneration or injury results in the tissue of the spinal nucleus seeping out and pressing against the spinal cord and spinal nerves. The symptoms of a herniated disk are like those of other back problems, yet can be even greater in their severity. Disk fluid can press upon the major nerve known as the sciatic nerve, resulting in shooting pain down the leg. Sometimes, even bladder control can be affected, meaning that you may not be able to control the urge to urinate.

Herniated disks require immediate rest and treatment by a professional physician. If the pain is acute, lying on the floor with the legs bent at the knees over a chair can bring some relief, as the position pushes the small of the back onto the floor where it is supported. Surgery may be required if the injury is severe. The results of surgery are generally good, and the wrestler will usually be able to return to training after

Damage to the disks between your vertebrae can cause severe pain, and may require surgery.

OVERUSE INJURIES

An overuse, or chronic, injury is caused by repeating the same action many times. This is not as serious as an acute injury, but any chronic problem may become worse if not acknowledged early on, so players should seek medical advice and treatment. Overuse injuries have both mental and physical symptoms:

- unusual tiredness or fatigue
- feeling very emotional, depressed, anxious, or stressed
- a lack of appetite
- an inability to sleep at night
- muscle soreness and cramps
- stiff, painful, or unstable joints
- problems getting parts of the body comfortable in bed at night
- painful tendons
- pain that shows no improvement for more than three days

only six to ten weeks. If surgery is not chosen, you may have to wear a back brace to stabilize the injury while it heals, and apply hot or cold packs, according to your doctor's instructions. A trained physical therapist may apply massage or **traction** to aid healing.

The muscles and joints of a wrestler's shoulders can become strained from overuse.

WRESTLING

TAKING CARE OF YOUR BACK

A strong back is not just a matter of training at the gym. How you sit, stand, lift, and carry yourself all help to maintain a healthy back.

- When sitting, push your bottom on the back of the chair and sit with your back straight, feet flat on the floor.
- When lifting heavy objects, do not bend from the waist over the object and lift it using your stomach and back muscles. Instead, first squat down next to the object and take hold of it. Next, straighten your back and look up. Finally, use your legs to push yourself into an upright position while holding the object close to your stomach.
- Do not let yourself become overweight; the excess weight will put a strain on your back muscles.
- Do regular flexibility and strength training to improve the overall muscle tone of your back.

Shoulder Problems

Apart from the neck and back, the shoulder is possibly the most vulnerable part of a wrestler. Wrestling techniques can strain the shoulders, and the shoulders' various muscles, **tendons**, ligaments, and joint structures can suffer from overuse injuries.

Typical shoulder problems include inflamed tendons and a torn rotator cuff (the series of muscles that hold the bony "ball" at the end of the arm in the shoulder socket). If the pain is relatively mild, you might not need to see a doctor. Instead, rest the shoulder for about a week. In the first few days of the injury, apply ice packs to reduce any swelling, and take painkillers such as ibuprofen, which has anti-inflammatory effects.

Gradually loosen up the shoulder with stretching and strengthening exercises. A rubber exercise band tied to a fixed object at the waist height can be a useful tool for rehabilitation. Stand upright and hold the end of the exercise band, then pull it slowly down toward your thighs, keeping the arm and back straight. Release the tension slowly. Repeat this exercise up to fifteen times.

If the injury is severe, see a doctor immediately. He may apply various treatments, including heat applications and ultrasound massage, and may even perform surgery. You may have to wear a sling for the arm, and you can expect to forego training for several months.

WRESTLING

5
Nutrition and Supplements

Understanding the Words

calories: *A measure of the amount of energy found in food and able to be used by the body.*

saturated fats: *A type of fats from animal products and found in some foods; they are known to raise cholesterol levels.*

rejuvenate: *To bring back to the original condition; to make something like it was when it was new or young.*

metabolism: *The chemical processes necessary for life that occur within the body, including breaking down substances to be used by the cells and creating new substances. The word metabolism is also used informally to refer to how quickly the body performs these processes.*

As they say, you are what you eat. The more balanced your diet is the more you'll be able to stay fit and exercise at your full potential. Simply being mindful of what you take into your body will aid you in training for wrestling. Athletes need to consume a proper blend of nutrients to ensure that their bodies and minds are performing at their full potential.

Nutritional wellness doesn't only mean eating healthy foods and checking each box at the grocery store for nutrients. When you eat, how much, and whether you use dietary supplements are all factors that are just as important as what you eat. Before dramatically changing your diet or taking supplements, you should speak to your doctor about these changes. An athlete shouldn't make up her own nutritional program.

You probably don't want to look like a sumo wrestler—so learn from a sumo wrestler's diet what NOT to do.

WRESTLING

Lessons from a Sumo Wrestler's Diet

Sumo wrestlers have a special diet they follow to bulk up—but must of us don't want to end up looking like sumo wrestlers! In America, our wrestlers are lean and muscular, so we want to do the opposite of the sumo-wrestler diet. The following are guidelines for what not to do when eating:

- Don't miss breakfast. Your body burns off extra fat slower without the kick-start in the morning breakfast provides.

- Don't starve yourself while you exercise. Without food, the body will conserve fat even during exercise.

- Don't take a nap immediately after eating, as this does not give your body the chance to burn off excess calories that you may have consumed.

- Don't eat your last meal late at night, and don't eat the most at your evening meal.

The principle behind a sumo wrestler's eating habits is to trick the brain into storing fat by ignoring the wants of the body. Instead, we should follow how our body works best. Eat a generous breakfast, then a large lunch when you're active. Eat dinner early at night and eat a light meal.

Caloric Intake

The average, active male eats 2,500 calories per day. A wrestler that needs to gain muscle mass while losing extra fat should be mindful of what he eats.

Know weight guidelines. Set yourself a goal for weight loss, and keep it always in your mind, but go for a weight goal that is realistic. Strategize. If you are slightly above a weight division, then safely attempt to gradually drop

Bananas are one of the few simple carbohydrates that are also high in nutritional value.

your weight to fit that division. If you find yourself in the middle of a weight division, concentrate on maintaining the same weight while increasing muscle weight vs. weight in fat.

Do the math. The principle behind the formula for weight-loss is simple: you want to burn more calories than you take in. If you do this, you have a calorie deficit and you lose weight. A deficit occurs when you lose more of something than you take in. So, if you want to lose two pounds (.9 kg) of fat per week, which is a healthy goal (do not attempt more than this), you need to eat 100 calories less per day and burn 1,000 calories more per day.

Timing: When to Eat

Make sure to eat three to four hours before a competition. When you eat before an event, make sure you stock up on carbohydrates. Avoid high-fat meals, or any kind of foods that contain **saturated fats**. Before a wrestling match, eat a liquid meal like a yogurt shake or sports drink. Do not eat any food less than an hour before an event. This will diminish your performance by cramping your stomach. However, you should drink water within this time before a match.

A Healthy Diet: What to Eat

CARBOHYDRATES

Carbohydrates provide energy to the body. Between 50 to 65 percent of a wrestler's diet should be carbohydrates. Think of carbohydrates (also known simply as "carbs") as the fuel that you need to keep your body running through workouts and tournaments. There are two types of carbohydrates: simple and complex.

Simple carbohydrates break down faster and provide a burst of energy but bring your body down fast. Usually, they are full of empty calories, food that doesn't enrich the body but has a high amount of calories. Most teenagers know and love simple carbohydrate foods—candy, soda, and other sweets—but an athlete should avoid these. While athletes should avoid empty-calorie foods at all times, they should especially steer clear of these foods before workouts to avoid a "crash" or feeling of a lack of energy while they work out.

Complex carbohydrates break down slower in the body and provide it with more nutrients. Vegetables, fruits, brown rice, whole-grain bread, beans, nuts, and cereal all contain complex carbohydrates. These complex carbohydrates give the body a longer-lasting boost of energy. Health professionals agree that switching from simple to complex carbohydrates is one of the smartest dietary choices a person can make. This can be as simple as buying whole-grain (brown) pasta instead of lighter kinds at the supermarket. Most complex carbohydrate foods are good sources of fiber, which makes the body feel more full. This also helps weight loss.

> **DID YOU KNOW?**
>
> Some fruits, such as bananas, are simple carbohydrates and are filled with other vitamins and minerals as well as fiber—but bananas are the exception and not the rule.

SIMPLE WAYS TO EAT COMPLEX CARBS

Keep these pointers in mind to make sure you're getting the right carbohydrates:

- Make at least half of your grains whole. Check the nutrition facts on bread, pasta, and cereal. Make sure the word "whole" is in the first ingredient and avoid the word "enriched." Because complex carbohydrates are popular, labels misleadingly call foods whole grain when they are not.
- Eat five servings of fruit, as well as five servings of vegetables, each day.

PROTEIN

Proteins are important chemicals found in all living things that are used to perform functions inside our body cells. Each protein is a long, folded chain-like molecule made up of "links" called amino acids. Our bodies break down proteins found in foods and build new proteins that give the body the building blocks needed to become strong. The best sources of proteins are meats and dairy products (like milk or cheese). Eggs and certain vegetables (such as soy beans and rice) are an excellent source of protein as well. A good rule of thumb for how much protein to eat is that the number of grams should be

Whole-grain breads like the ones shown here are better choices than white bread, since they contain complex carbohydrates, which will give your body longer-lasting energy.

WRESTLING IS WHAT COUNTS

Getting into a lower weight division is only one way of becoming more competitive. It is not the point of wrestling. The number-one goal is to win matches. You are not in a weight-loss competition; you are training to take down an opponent in the ring. Keep your thoughts on winning a match, not just losing weight.

equal to about one-third of your weight in pounds. For example, a 200-pound (90.7 kilograms) person should eat about 70 grams of protein every day. Or a 120-pound person (54.4 kilograms) should have 40 grams of proteins.

FATS

Although fats are often considered to be foods we should avoid, they help repair the body and can be used as sources of energy. Healthy skin, teeth, and hair require a steady diet of fats. Also nerve-functions require a certain amount of fat. Fatty foods should, however, take up no more than 25 percent of caloric intake. The kind of fat one consumes makes a difference, though; not all fats are alike.

Fats can be classified as: polyunsaturated, monounsaturated fats, and saturated fats. Unsaturated fat is good for the body, and saturated fats are best avoided. Monounsaturated fats (MUFA) are found in foods such as nuts, avocados, canola, and olive oil. These foods help contribute to weight loss. Polyunsaturated fats such as salmon, fish oil, corn, and soy lower cholesterol. Omega 3 fatty acids are polyunsaturated and are found in fish oil. Fish oil can offer benefits such as healthier heart performance and cancer prevention. Omega 3 can even improve mental health.

On the other hand, meat, dairy, eggs, and seafood all contain saturated fats, and too much of these are not healthy for your body. Other oils such as coconut oil and palm oil also have "bad" saturated fat.

Trans fats are created by scientists to preserve foods longer on the shelf. Many packaged foods like chips and microwavable popcorn contain trans fats. Fries from fast-food restaurants commonly put trans fats in their foods. The health effects of taking trans fat are numerous and range from obesity and heart disease to infertility in women and even Alzheimer's.

Since trans fats are particularly dangerous, eat only packaged products that provide this information.

All these saturated fats add to a sluggish feeling after they are eaten. Any kind of fat takes from three to five hours to fully digest, so stock up on complex carbohydrates for energy instead of fatty foods.

WATER

Water has been called the most important of all nutrients. The body is made up of 60 percent water, and all parts of the body depend on water to function.

Water is so important that the body can only go for 48 hours without it, whereas it can survive for weeks without food.

By hydrating (filling with water) ourselves, we **rejuvenate** all parts of our body, including the brain. Water transports nutrients around the body and helps regulate temperature and **metabolism**. You should drink water before, during and after exercise. Wrestlers should drink eight glasses of water a day.

By hydrating, a wrestler is being healthier and also prepping her body for optimum performance to gain muscle mass. Drinking water gives you more strength and endurance. Even a small amount of dehydration can decrease strength by 15 percent, so to maximize workout intensity, an athlete needs to be hydrated. The entire process of muscle gain is aided by water. Water also helps protect joints, by assisting our body in lubricating the joints between our bones.

Invest in a water bottle and keep it filled, so that you can maintain your body's hydration.

TIPS FOR EATING

How we eat can be as important as what we eat. Here are some useful tips on eating meals:

- Eat slowly. By eating your food at a leisurely pace, your meal will feel more filling after you are done.
- Chew your food. It may sound too basic, but by chewing your food slowly you stimulate secretions in the mouth, which start up the digestive process.
- Graze. This means eating smaller amounts more frequently than the more conventional habit of eating three large meals a day.

Eating Disorders and Wrestling

An 2004 article for the Princeton University student newspaper revealed the dangers of eating disorders. They interviewed a man (called Paul in the article; he did not reveal his real name) who became trapped by eating disorders once he got to college and began wrestling at Ivy-League level. In high school, he had already worked himself down to 5 percent body-fat—but the healthy range of body fat is 13 to 16 percent for men. By the time he was wrestling at the college level, he had a full-fledged eat disorder.

For a wrestler to develop an eating disorder in college is not uncommon. An anonymous friend of Paul's stated, "[at Princeton] 95 percent of the wrestlers have had an eating disorder at one time." Even more dangerous is the notion that if the unhealthy eating habits are formed for a sport, it's okay. Paul said, "I told myself, 'this isn't bulimia, because I'm doing it for wrestling.'"

Traditionally, eating disorders were nearly exclusively a female problem, but they have begun to be more common among males. The nonprofit organization Eating Disorders Awareness and Prevention, Inc., estimated in 2004 that 5 to 10 million women and one million men in the United States suffered from eating disorders. Male eating disorders increased by 30 percent since 1972. The pressure to be lighter is even worse for wrestlers because of the emphasis on weight-loss to be competitive.

Eating disorders are psychological problems that were once thought to affect only women. More men, however, are experiencing this problem, and wrestlers may be particularly at risk of becoming obsessed with their weight.

WARNING SIGNS OF AN EATING DISORDER

Eating disorders and wrestling don't mix. If you see any of these signs coming up in your eating habits or your behavior, then seriously consider getting help:

- You feel frequently tired. If you feel you never have energy because you're not eating enough, this is a serious sign that you are suffering for an eating disorder.
- You have an irregular eating schedule; for instance, you don't eat anything until late at night.
- Your body does not hold onto heat as well. People suffering from eating disorders will wear heavier-than-appropriate clothing.

Paul was at a low point at Princeton: "You just feel disgusted with yourself. . . . I had no sex drive." Wrestlers start unhealthy eating habits for the benefit of their sport—but in the end, their sport suffers as well. "My wrestling started going completely downhill," Paul said. This is the norm. Studies found it is nearly impossible to have both an eating disorder and a normal athletic life or social life. Eating disorders destroy athletes' careers. Even worse, sometimes they destroy athletes' lives.

Nutritional Supplements

In a perfect world, wrestlers could get every necessary nutrient from eating food directly. Unfortunately, even well-monitored diets do not always give our bodies needed vitamins and minerals. Dietary supplements should only be used to give our body what it cannot supply itself through food.

VITAMIN TABLETS

Vitamins come in many forms. Some provide only one vitamin or mineral that makes up for a neglected nutrient. There are also multivitamins that offer a combination of vitamins and minerals that are needed daily. A good multivitamin should have close to 100 percent of daily-required minerals and vitamins and should be taken at recommended dosages with water near mealtime. In general, an athlete should drink eight glasses of water every day to get the most out of vitamins.

Never take more than the recommended amount. Any excess vitamin intake will leave the body—or even worse, be stored in the kidneys. It is even possible to overdose on vitamins.

Some supplements are infused with more vitamins than are required daily. For instance, B6 vitamins are sold in one-gram quantities, but the body only needs up to 2 milligrams per day. You should only take a tablet of this amount of dosage every two days. An overdose of vitamin B6 can cause sensory and motor control loss. Other vitamins have equally harmful effects if taken in excess. Vitamin E overdoses cause blood clots, tumors, fatigue, and reproductive problems. While extra Vitamin C flushes out the body, Vitamin A stores in the kidneys and causes fatigue and dry and itchy skin. When it comes to dietary supplements, there is such thing as too much of a good thing!

CREATINE

Creatine is an attractive dietary supplement for weightlifters because it is believed to give more energy and power during a workout. Creatine is a protein that is naturally found in your body's muscle cells. When taken in larger doses than is found in the body, creatine has the effect of increasing the rate of protein synthesis within your cells. This means that you will have more energy for lifting weights.

Creatine does not have the same effect for everyone, however. Between 20 to 30 percent of the general population will not respond to creatine supplements. And athletes who are seventeen or younger should never take creatine. Always talk to your doctor before taking any nutritional supplements.

PROTEIN SUPPLEMENTS

Getting enough protein from the food you eat can be difficult sometimes—but to refuel your body,

This bodybuilding supplement contains protein and creatine, as well as vitamins and other supplements. It may improve your ability to build muscles, but if you are under 18, you should not take it until you are older.

WRESTLING

eating protein immediately after a workout is recommended. Most people do not want to cook a meal right after they have pumped iron at the gym, protein shakes can be a convenient alternative. Many shakes contain blends of proteins, carbohydrates, fats, and vitamins.

Remember that protein shakes are useful as dietary supplements, not dietary replacements. You can get plenty of nutrients from a balanced diet that can't be replaced by artificial protein shakes.

Ginseng root has been used for centuries in Asia as a natural stimulant.

GINSENG

Ginseng is a natural herb found in Asia that is said to increase alertness and energy. Many experts do not recommend ginseng for bodybuilding because higher dosages may increase body temperature, unnecessarily increase the heart rate, and possibly cause insomnia. No scientific evidence supports ginseng's use in athletics. Most of the studies that showed positive outcomes did not use credible methods. In studies where one group was given real ginseng and others were given pills that did nothing (called placebos), there was almost no difference between those who took the placebo and those who took the real ginseng.

6

The Dangers of Performance-Enhancing Drugs

Understanding the Words

debilitating: *Making you weaker or damaging your health.*

stimulating: *Encouraging something to happen.*

euphoria: *An exaggerated feeling of happiness, confidence, and well-being.*

Many young athletes feel intense pressure to perform well. Sometimes, they may feel tempted to turn to chemical enhancements to reach a level of performance they would not normally be capable of. This is never legal, and is almost always dangerous, but nevertheless, some wrestlers feel compelled to participate in performance-enhancing drug use.

What Are Drugs?

In general, a drug is anything you place into your body that changes your body's chemistry in some way. Drugs can be useful or beneficial, such as the tablets you might take when you have a headache or antibiotics developed to fight diseases. Steroids are drugs useful for certain people with **debilitating** conditions that cause their muscles to waste away, and steroids can also be used to decrease inflam-

Drugs can be either beneficial or harmful (and the same pill could have both effects, depending on dosage and how it is taken). Basically, a drug is any substance designed to create a chemical change within the body.

mation. However, many drugs, including anabolic steroids, can have serious negative effects on your health.

Steroids

The most common performance enhancers are anabolic steroids. Athletes use steroids for many reasons. We live in a culture of easy fixes, and it's hard to resist the allure of being able to bench-press an additional fifty pounds (22.6 kilograms) simply by taking a pill regularly. Another factor that contributes to steroid abuse is their availability. *Sports Weekly* held a discussion with high school athletes in the Washington area and found out that steroids were being openly used around the locker room and even the cafeteria.

Anabolic steroids are drugs that chemically resemble androgenic hormones such as testosterone. Steroids work by **stimulating** receptors found in muscle cells that cause stronger muscle growth during a workout. Despite this beneficial result, there are at least three important reasons not to take steroids:

• Steroids ruin reproductive functions. Testosterone is essential for producing sperm and maintaining a healthy sex drive and sexual function. The natural production of testosterone is impaired by the abuse of steroids. When a wrestler abuses steroids, they disrupt the way his reproductive system functions. Shrunken testicles, decreased sperm count, impotence, decreased sex drive, and infertility can occur because of steroid abuse. Some studies even suggest that some of these effects do not go away even after the wrestler has stopped taking steroids.

• Steroids cloud the mind. While scientific studies have not verified that "roid rage" (an uncontrollable violent urge) as it is portrayed in the media is an effect of taking steroids, scientific studies have found a higher amount of irritability, aggressiveness, euphoria, hyperactivity, and recklessness in steroid abusers. They have also found that steroid abusers suffer from depression.

Wrestling is not an "easy" sport—so it makes sense that there are no easy shortcuts to achieving the body you need to excel in wrestling. It takes self-discipline and hard work to be a wrestler, but the rewards are well worth the effort.

• Steroid abuse is illegal. Since 1991, possession of illegally obtained steroids carries a maximum penalty of one year in prison and a minimum fine of $1,000 for a first drug offense. The maximum penalty for selling steroids is five years in prison and a $250,000 fine for a first offender. If caught again, the timeframe and fees double. There are also laws for schools, and student drug testing is a legitimate form of a school drug prevention program. Most weightlifting competitions ban steroid use.

Diuretics

Diuretics are drugs that cause you to get rid of extra water from your body, which makes you weigh less. Wrestling is a sport with "weigh-ins," because classes of competition are based on weight. Because of this, wrestlers often use diuretics to make them weigh just enough less to qualify for a different division. The pressure to lose weight fast is great, and diuretics are an easy-fix way to lose extra weight by losing water.

Diuretics are also used to mask the abuse of other substances like steroids. By taking a diuretic, the body flushes out many of the traces of other drugs that are abused. Because of this, many officiators at wrestling competitions test for diuretic abuse.

Diuretics are dangerous; taking them will deplete your body of more than just weight. These drugs hinder the body's ability to function normally—and this is the opposite of what a wrestler needs. By depleting the body of water, potassium drops, causing heart problems. Headaches, nausea, and dizziness also follow as a result of the body losing unusual mounts of liquid. Fatal conditions such as kidney damage can occur because of diuretic abuse.

Closing Words

"That which does not destroy, strengthens," said Friederich Nietzsche. Wrestling is a sport where athletes use pain to grow strong.

There is no effortless way to lose weight and be healthy. Why would there be? Wrestling an opponent into submission isn't easy either. Neither is spending hours at the gym that could be spent having a good time with friends. All aspects of wrestling require dedication.

Taking performance-enhancing drugs is an attempt to trick our bodies into being fit, but as this chapter shows, there is no easy fix. Instead of teaching ourselves to take strength from hardship, drugs destroy our lives.

The benefits of wrestling go farther than just winning fights or being fit. Wrestling teaches us discipline and resilience: the ability to stick to things even when they are tough. We don't just want to survive in life. We want to win.

Further Reading

Chapman, Mike. *Wrestling Tough*. Champagne, Ill.: Human Kinetics, 2005.

Couture, Randy, Erich Krauss, and Glen Cordoza. *Wrestling for Fighting: The Natural Way.* Las Vegas, Nev.: Victory Belt Publishing, 2007.

Gunter, Joseph C. *The Effects and Risks of Extreme Weight Loss on the Body of a Wrestler: A Report of a Senior Study.* Frederick, Md.: PublishAmerica, 2007.

Price, Robert G. *The Ultimate Guide to Weight Training for Wrestling*. Cleveland, Ohio: Price World Enterprises, 2003.

Ryan, Thomas and Julie Sampson. *Beginning Wrestling.* New York: Sterling, 2002.

Welker, William. *The Wrestling Drill Book*. Champagne, Ill.: Human Kinetics, 2005.

Whitsett, Lisa. *Beneath the Armor of an Athlete: Real Strength on the Wrestling Mat.* Terre Haut, Ind.: Wish Publishing, 2003.

Find Out More on the Internet

Freestyle Wrestling, United States Olympic Education Center
webb.nmu.edu/SportsUSOEC/Sports/FreestyleWrestling/Home.shtml

InterMat, RevWrestling
www.intermatwrestling.com

National Collegiate Wrestling Association
www.ncwa.net

Takedown Techniques, Today! Fitness
www.todayfitness.net/wrestling/takedowns

USA Wrestling
www.themat.com

"What is Greco-Roman Wrestling?"
www.themmaforums.com/articles/greco-roman wrestling/greco roman wrestling.html

Wrestling USA Magazine
www.wrestlingusa.com

Disclaimer

The websites listed on this page were active at the time of publication. The publisher is not responsible for websites that have changed their address or discontinued operation since the date of publication. The publisher will review and update the websites upon each reprint.

WRESTLING

Bibliography

Douglas, Bobby. "Nutrition Guidelines," bobbydouglas.com/insight.
html#Nutrition%20Guidelines (30 April 2010).

Graham, Elyse. "College men increasingly suffer from eating disorders,
partly pressured by athletics," *The Daily Princetonian* www.dailyprinceton-
ian.com/2004/10/14/11087/ (3 May 2010).

Swertfager, Bill. "Wrestling Weight Control System: 38 Diet Tips & Facts for
Wrestlers," www.sectiononewrestling.com/documents/wrestling_weight_
control_diet_facts.html (29 April 2010).

Index

WRESTLING

Picture Credits

Albix; Fotolia: p. 50
Carr, Dreier; Creative Commons: pp. 18, 31, 38
Cervo, Diego; Fotolia: p. 52
Creative Commons: pp. 33, 70, 75
Ellington; Creative Commons: p. 35
Eythorsson; Creative Commons: p. 15
Farino, Marcella; Creative Commons: p. 24
Flippo, Michael; Fotolia: p. 78
FotoDawg, Creative Commons: p. 73
Four Tildes, Creative Commons: p. 68
Imagery Majestic; Fotolia: p. 44
Jastrow; Creative Commons: p. 12
Kallhardt, Marius; Creative Commons: p. 10
Kaulitzki, Sebastian; Dreamstime: p. 47
Lecko, Peter; Fotolia: p. 63
London England, Fotolia: p. 57
Mike1024, Creative Commons: p. 81
Richardfabi, Creative Commons: p. 82
Tomus, Sebastian; Fotolia: p. 86
Traveling Lens, Fotolia: p. 58
U.S. Airforce: p. 24
U.S. Department of Defense: p. 21
U.S. Navy: pp. 43, 49, 88
Zimmytws, Fotolia: p. 61

To the best knowledge of the publisher, all images not specifically credited are in the public domain. If any image has been inadvertently uncredited, please notify Harding House Publishing Service, 220 Front Street, Vestal, New York 13850, so that credit can be given in future printings.

WRESTLING

About the Author and the Consultants

J.S. McIntosh is a writer living in upstate New York. He graduated from Binghamton University with a degree in English literature. He enjoys making music on his laptop, playing poker, and being a literacy volunteer. Currently, he writes on topics ranging from military history to health and fitness.

Susan Saliba, Ph.D., is a senior associate athletic trainer and a clinical instructor at the University of Virginia in Charlottesville, Virginia. A certified athletic trainer and licensed physical therapist, Dr. Saliba provides sports medicine care, including prevention, treatment, and rehabilitation for the varsity athletes at the university. Dr. Saliba is a member of the national Athletic Trainers' Association Educational Executive Committee and its Clinical Education Committee.

Eric Small, M.D., a Harvard-trained sports medicine physician, is a nationally recognized expert in the field of sports injuries, nutritional supplements, and weight management programs. He is author of *Kids & Sports* (2002) and is Assistant Clinical professor of pediatrics, Orthopedics, and Rehabilitation Medicine at Mount Sinai School of Medicine in New York. He is also Director of the Sports Medicine Center for Young Athletes at Blythedale Children's Hospital in Valhalla, New York. Dr. Small has served on the American Academy of Pediatrics Committee on Sports Medicine, where he develops national policy regarding children's medical issues and sports.

WRESTLING